THIS WAS THE WOODHEAD ROUTE

CW01653249

S.R. BATTY

LONDON

IAN ALLAN LTD

Cover: **Nos 76.021 and 76.008 seen at Penistone with coal empties on 13 February 1981.** *C. Richard Wilby*

First published 1981

ISBN 0 9110 1140 0

All rights reserved. No part of this book may be reproduced or transmitted in any form or by any means, electronic or mechanical, including photocopying, recording or by any information storage and retrieval system, without permission from the Publisher in writing.

© Ian Allan Ltd 1981

Published by Ian Allan Ltd, Shepperton, Surrey, and printed by Ian Allan Printing Ltd at their works at Coombelands in Runnymede, England.

Introduction

Many famous main line railway routes have had their scenery, operation and sometimes, sadly, their decline, well illustrated in recent times. The Manchester-Penistone-Sheffield route and associated Penistone-Wath freight-only line have been somewhat neglected in this respect, and in this album I have set out to show some of the diversity of operations, variety of landscape and notable features of the routes as seen during the past 40 years. Landscapes vary from industrialised conurbations to rich farmland and bleak moors, with the line negotiating gradients and curves over almost its entire length. The motive power stud has been drawn from locomotives of mainly MSLR/GCR/LNER origin, and included many types, from the graceful 'Jersey Lily' Atlantics and 'Director' 4-4-0s to the functional LNER-designed electric locomotives and BR diesels. Perhaps civil engineering works provide the route's most famous features; the three Woodhead tunnels and the electrification works being milestones of railway achievement.

The line was born during late 1835, when poor communications between the booming cities of Manchester and Sheffield prompted local industrialists to engage Charles Vignoles to engineer a railway line to be known as the Sheffield, Ashton-under-Lyne and Manchester Railway, using locomotive haulage throughout. Parliamentary authorisation was received in 1838, and the entire route had been staked out by the spring of the following year. From the outset it was realised that heavy expenditure would be required in tunnelling at Woodhead, and to save money a single-bore tunnel only was planned, at an estimated cost of £60,000. Several other economies had to be made during the planning and construction, but this proved to be the most short-sighted of the measures taken. Much has been written about the appalling living and working conditions which made the tunnel site a byword for exploitation, disease and debauchery. Suffice it to say here that by the time it was finally opened for traffic on 22 December 1845, its 3 miles 22yd length had claimed 26 lives, injured 140, and cost the SA&MR a total of £200,000 – more than three times the estimated cost. Very soon after regular operation over the line had settled down, it became clear that the tunnel was a major bottleneck and would prevent any future traffic increase. To alleviate the problem a contract for a second, parallel, tunnel to carry a separate up line was placed in February 1847. Traffic was expected to increase rapidly in the near future as the SA&MR had, by amalgamation, become part of the Manchester, Sheffield and Lincolnshire Railway, with routes stretching across the Yorkshire coalfield to Gainsborough and Grimsby. With this lucrative coal traffic in view, in 1848 the MSLR obtained powers for a line to Barnsley via Silkstone, Dodworth and Summer Lane to a joint station with the Lancashire & Yorkshire Railway at Barnsley Exchange. Shortage of money delayed the start of the project until 1852, and the single line was eventually opened in 1857.

Meanwhile, in 1850, the Huddersfield & Sheffield Junction Railway had been opened and this joined the MSLR line at Penistone, approaching on a 330yd long viaduct which was 98ft high. The MSLR's new station at Sheffield Victoria was opened on 15 September 1851, and the first traffic passed through the new 3 mile 24yd long tunnel at Woodhead on 2 February 1852. Twenty-eight lives had been lost during its construction, and most of these had fallen victim to the great cholera epidemic of 1849. The basic railway network of the area was now complete, and traffic built up steadily. In 1862 a Bessemer steelworks was opened at Penistone adjacent to the junction with the H&SJR. The works generated much traffic until it was closed and demolished during the Depression of the 1930s. The Barnsley line which had opened in 1857 was doubled in 1871, and the present station at Penistone was erected in 1874 to the east of the original station, which became a goods depot. The amount of coal traffic passing through Barnsley Exchange was, by this time, causing serious congestion, and to relieve this situation the Wentworth incline was built. The ex-South Yorkshire Railway Worsborough branch line from Barnsley to Moor End Colliery was extended by over 2 miles, over a 1 in 40 gradient, to meet the Barnsley line at West Silkstone Junction. Two tunnels 74yd and 289yd long, were needed, and the extension was opened on 2 August 1880.

The later years of the nineteenth century were hectic times for the MSLR. The London 'extension' was progressing, and through passenger services from Manchester and the West Riding demanded greater track capacity along the Woodhead route. Extensive loops were installed during 1895/96 at Neepsend, Woodhead, Torside, and Valehouse to meet this need. To promote a more grand and unified image, the MSLR became the Great Central Railway from 1 August 1897.

The new company immediately set about dealing with the ever-increasing freight traffic, and laid out two gravity marshalling yards, one at Wath, near Mexborough, and one at Dunford, at the eastern approach to Woodhead tunnel. These were opened in 1907 and 1901 respectively. To shorten the signalling block section between Woodhead and Dunford Bridge through the tunnel a signalbox was opened in 1902 actually within the gloomy depths of the up tunnel. Signalmen were reluctant to work even a reduced shift of six hours in the new cabin, where tail lamps were almost impossible to see for smoke, and drivers had difficulty in restarting heavy trains if they were stopped within the bore on the rising 1 in 201 gradient. The cabin was closed in 1909.

By 1914 all traffic was being handled by locomotives built since 1900 and designed by the GCR Locomotive Engineer, John G. Robinson. Freight was hauled by 0-6-0 'Pom-Poms', 0-8-0 'Tinies' and the standard GCR Class 9K 2-8-0, soon to be famous as the 'ROD' class. Passenger trains were usually hauled by the graceful 'Atlantics' and the new 'Director' 4-4-0s, with the new 4-6-0s appearing on all express workings. The first thoughts of electrification came in 1913 when Robinson visited the United States and saw some early 1,500V d.c. systems in operation. He was sufficiently impressed to consider its use on the Worsborough line, but eventually the capital cost of the equipment saw the scheme ruled out, and the heavy coal trains had to labour on with steam power for a further 40 years. A design for a three-cylinder 0-10-2 banking engine for the line was produced, but the locomotive never materialised.

The London and North Eastern Railway took over the lines at the Grouping in 1923, and to assist the movement of coal traffic acquired the country's first main-line Beyer-Garratt locomotive in 1925. No 2395 was a 2-8-8-2 of 72,940lb starting tractive effort, designed to be available for banking duty for 20 out of every 24 hours. Respirators were provided for the crew to use through the Silkstone tunnels, where the speed of an 850ton train was usually below 10mph.

Electrification was examined again in 1926, this time for the entire route from Manchester to Sheffield and Wath, but was shelved due to other pressing commitments on the LNER. The scheme was revived in 1936, and with some alterations formed the basis of the system which was eventually completed. The two Woodhead tunnels were to be refurbished, and the entire cost of the conversion was estimated at £2.5million. Much of the overhead catenary west of Woodhead had been erected and a start had been made at Gorton Works on the construction of 70 Bo-Bo locomotives when the war stopped all work in 1940. The first Bo-Bo No 6701, was completed in 1939 and tested in the Altrincham area. It was then placed in store until the war ended, and in 1947 it was loaned to the Netherlands Railways which at that time were desperately short of locomotives. While in Holland it earned the nickname *Tommy*, which it subsequently carried on special commemorative nameplates. During the late 1950s all the Class EM2 Co-Cos and several of the 'EM1' Bo-Bos were given names. All were removed in the early 1970s.

In 1944 the scheme was again reviewed, and the LNER decided to open out Thurgoland tunnel (between Penistone and Wortley) and to construct an electric motive power depot at Reddish in Manchester. Work restarted in 1946, but geological problems precluded the planned work at Thurgoland and a second 350yd tunnel had to be driven alongside the original, which then became the up tunnel. At Woodhead, the planned refurbishment of the tunnels was also proving problematic. Almost a century of steam operation combined with a wartime backlog of maintenance had left both bores barely serviceable, with mortar falling from the linings and the permanent way being attacked by the acid-laden atmosphere. Initial week-long possessions of both tunnels became nine-month occupations, with still no end to the repair work in sight. The LNER believed that even if the work could be completed, further major reconstruction would be necessary within ten years. The decision was then made to construct a new, double-track tunnel and to close the original bores on completion of the work. Parliamentary approval was given in 1947, and the estimated cost was £2.8million. Work started in February 1949, the new bore being to the south of the existing tunnels. Steam locomotives were to be banned from using the tunnel, thus allowing ordinary Portland cement to be used for the lining.

On the motive power front the original order for 70 Class EM1 Bo-Bo locomotives was reduced to 58, but

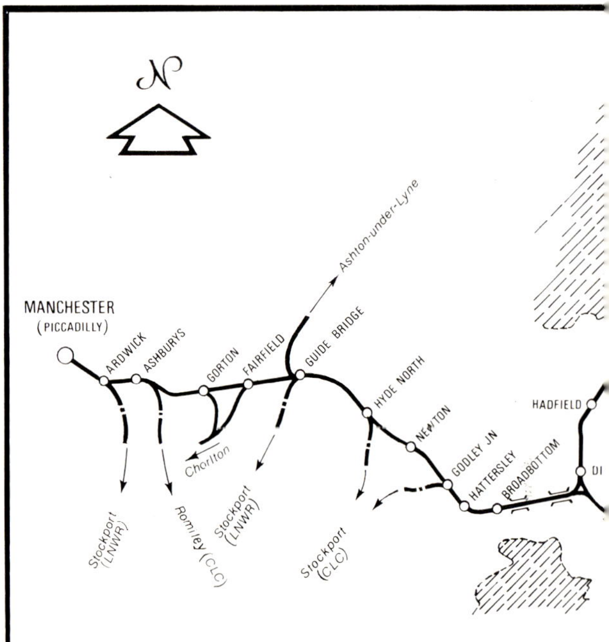

27 larger, more powerful Co-Co locomotives were ordered to handle express passenger traffic. But by 1950 however, the cost of the electrification had risen to £12.25million, and some economies were made. The Class EM2 Co-Co order was reduced to seven units, and a plan to extend the electrification from Trafford Park to Manchester Central was abandoned. Work then proceeded in three stages, and Stage One, from Wath to Dunford, was completed on 2 February 1952 when all freight traffic over this section was turned over to electric traction. The 142 minute allowance for up to four steam locomotives with an 850ton train became a 66 minute trip for two of the new 'EM1' Bo-Bos. The steam/electric changeover was performed at Penistone. At Woodhead the new tunnel works were completed during October 1953 and opened to traffic on 3 June 1954, having incurred a total cost of £4.25million.

Stage Two was thus completed, with a changeover still being required at Penistone for Sheffield traffic. Stage Three, bringing full electric working into Sheffield Victoria was completed on 20 September 1954, and the freight sidings at Rotherwood were reached early in 1955. Between Manchester London Road and Sheffield Victoria the express passenger train timing for the 41¼ miles was reduced from 65 minutes to 56 minutes by the new 'EM2' locomotives.

The two cities were connected by a system which, although it was already being superseded by more modern forms of electrification, was nevertheless a showpiece for British Railways. Some rationalisation took place during the remaining years of the 1950s; Wortley closed to passengers from 2 May 1955, Crowden closed entirely from 4 February 1957 and stations at Wadsley Bridge, Oughtybridge, Deepcar, Silkstone, Dodworth, Summer Lane and Wath (Central) closed on 14 June 1959. The Winter 1959/60 timetable saw the first fall of the axe on the original GCR lines with the withdrawal of all through passenger services from Marylebone to stations beyond Nottingham. So ended the famous 'South Yorkshireman', 10.00 from Bradford (Exchange) and 16.50 return from Marylebone. An hourly interval service was introduced between Sheffield and Manchester, but it is perhaps from this point that the line's fortunes declined. Woodhead station closed to goods traffic on 1 July 1963, followed by Dunford Bridge on 16 December. Hazlehead Bridge, which had seen only goods traffic since March 1950, closed completely on 4 April 1964, and Woodhead saw its last passengers on 27 July 1964. The Beeching Report cast gloom over the passenger services, and in October 1965 24 trains per day were diverted to run from Sheffield (Midland) via the Hope Valley line to Manchester.

Freight traffic, however, was seen as ideally suited to the line, and during 1965 the electrification was extended to the newly-opened Tinsley marshalling yard at Sheffield. The new equipment was designed to allow future operation at 6.25kV, then the new standard, and surely an optimistic sign for the future. British Railways then proposed withdrawal of the Manchester-Sheffield passenger service from 5 June 1967, but the resulting outcry prompted an enquiry which took two years to reach its conclusion. Meanwhile, BR carried out experimental through running to Penistone with the Manchester-Hadfield emus. Here they were to connect with the recently introduced Huddersfield-Sheffield

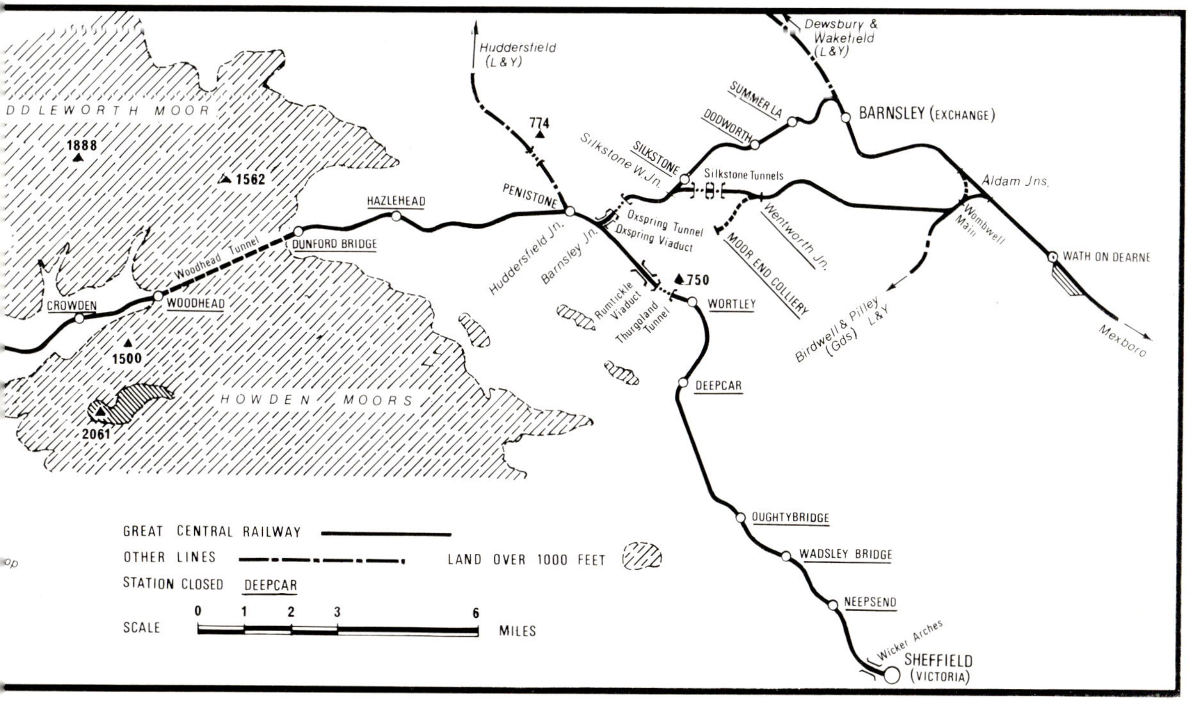

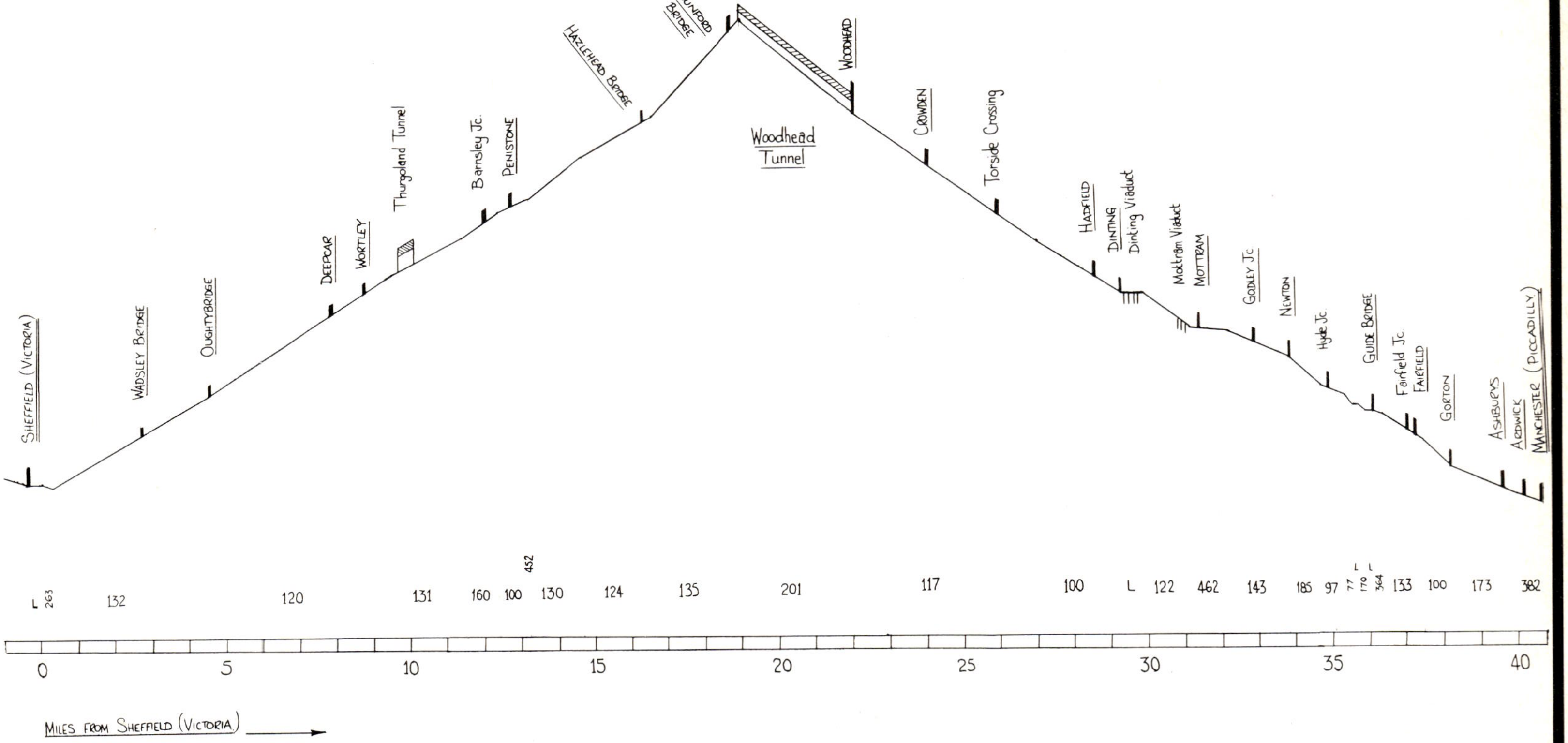

Sheffield (Victoria) — Manchester (Piccadilly)

Victoria dmus, but tunnel clearances proved to be too tight and the idea was dropped. In August 1969 the Minister of Transport decided to allow withdrawal of the through passenger service to increase line capacity for the large amount of freight traffic, quoted as 100 trains per day in each direction. Under the new BR classification system the 'EM1s' became Class 76 and a number were fitted with jumper connections so that they could work in multiple. With their passenger duties gone, the 'EM2' locomotives were sold to the Netherlands Railways (NS) where some of them remain in use. The 18.40 Manchester Piccadilly – Sheffield Victoria and 22.15 return were the last passenger trains to run on 5 January 1970, from which date Dunford Bridge and Sheffield Victoria stations were closed, and the MSW line platforms at Penistone became disused.

How did the route appear in 1980, to the driver of the westbound steel or coal train? The shell of Sheffield Victoria remained, its decaying platforms, kiosks, offices and waiting rooms providing a lonely, desolate atmosphere to a once hectic centre of railway operation. Barely a mile beyond the platform ends, the line started a 4-mile climb at 1 in 132 through a heavily industrialised area and closely followed the River Don. Along the valley side past Wadsley Bridge, the surroundings gradually became more urban towards Oughtybridge, where the gradient stiffened to 1 in 120. Woodland provided a gentle backdrop past Deepcar, where exchange sidings for Stocksbridge Steelworks were situated, and on to Wortley. Here the valley opens out to give views of farmland, broken only by drystone walls and small patches of woodland. Just east of Thurgoland tunnels the gradient eased to 1 in 131, and this continued for the two miles on to Barnsley Juntion, east of Penistone.

At this point the Worsborough line diverged. It left Wath-on-Dearne and headed north-west to Aldam Junction on rising gradients of 1 in 424 to 1 in 217. Here, the line turned left, away from the Doncaster-Barnsley line and climbed steeply at 1 in 63 round to Wombwell Main Junction. A large area of sidings, latterly empty, were passed on the up side as the line first dropped and then gently climbed around the southern outskirts of Barnsley. The coal mines were left behind as the line climbed at 1 in 106, crossed the M1 motorway and approached the remains of Wentworth Junction, where the formidable 2 miles uphill at 1 in 40 commenced. The all-out efforts of four steam locomotives grinding uphill with a reluctant coal train must have been rather out of place amid the agricultural world which surrounded the railway! The two Silkstone tunnels were taken on a gradual curve, and then the line seemed almost to fall over the summit onto the relatively easy 1 in 100 at West Silkstone Junction, where the original Barnsley route via Dodworth trailed in from the right. After descending through Oxspring tunnel and crossing the viaduct the main line from Sheffield was joined at Barnsley Junction. Penistone station platforms are still largely intact, although the roofs were removed in 1979 and

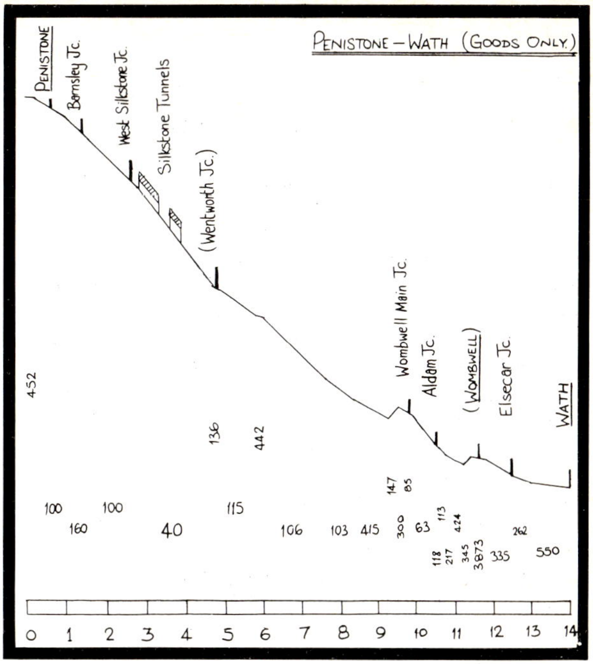

most of the remaining offices were unused at the end except for BR maintenance teams and a small local enterprise. Passengers for the Huddersfield-Sheffield (Midland) Paytrains must wait on the exposed branch platform, adjacent to the viaduct which heads northwards to Denby Dale. Even these last vestiges of Penistone station are under threat of closure. The westward climb continued at 1 in 130 and through a short cutting to Thurlstone, where open views of the countryside were to be seen once more. A wide, sweeping curve brought the line over Shore Hall Crossing and past Bullhouse curve, where the climb steepened to 1 in 124. At Hazlehead Bridge, nothing remained of the former station, and the scenery changed to heather and bog as the line crossed Thurlstone Moor. The closed and levelled yards at Dunford (East) were passed, and below the River Don could be seen, reduced to stream-width as it approached its source at Winscar Reservoir above Dunford Bridge station. The original lines and approaches to the Woodhead tunnels could be clearly seen, but at the platform ends an embankment separated old and new entrances. The summit of the climb was reached at the tunnel mouth, where trains plunged into 2 miles of darkness on a falling gradient of 1 in 201. It steepened to 1 in 117 at the western exit, where the original tunnel portals were also visible and passed Woodhead Station to begin the descent through Longdendale. Initially straight alignment was followed by gentle curvature as the line passed high, bleak moorland surrounding the reservoirs of Woodhead, Torside, Rhodeswood and Valehouse. The remains of Crowden station were passed, and Torside crossing was the first sign of habitation since Dunford. At Valehouse the descent steepened to 1 in 100 for the 2.5 miles to Dinting, where commuters can catch the

Piccadilly-Glossop emus which still use the remaining section of the line to Manchester. Immediately off the ends of the well-kept platforms is Dinting viaduct, 1,455ft long, which carries the line 121ft above Dinting Vale and on to Mottram. Exchange sidings here are used for the merry-go-round coal trains, and Class 47 diesel power is often evident. After traversing Mottram viaduct above the River Etherow, trains descend through Broadbottom and Hattersley (opened in 1978 for commuter traffic) to Godley Junction, where there were more exchange sidings. From here the mgr trains would continue their journey to Fiddler's Ferry power station via the ex-CLC route to Stockport, which heads due west from the station. The line descends through Newton and passes Hyde (North) on a sudden drop of 1 in 97, where another ex-CLC line from Stockport trails in from the down side. The Manchester industrial scene is now fully evident, and Guide Bridge station and yards lie at the heart of a maze of ex-LNWR and ex-GCR lines. The descent through Fairfield, Gorton and Ashburys (which was the limit of Class 76 operation westwards) is at 1 in 100 to 1 in 173, and from Ardwick the line runs parallel to the LM 25kV a.c. system for the remaining mile into Piccadilly station.

For the last 10 years the Woodhead route has carried mgr coal trains, oil, liquefied gases, steel, sand, and chemicals. The lack of junctions and stations ensured fairly rapid running times for these loads, but the number of trains fell drastically from the 1970 level. During the 1970s BR made known their desire to close the line between Deepcar and Dinting, basing the proposal mainly on the lack of locally-generated traffic and the high cost of maintaining or converting the obsolete electrification equipment. Tremendous opposition was voiced, as it was in the 1960s, but this time by trade unions and local MPs. Many people see the outcome as a foregone conclusion, but the debates, arguments and counter-arguments are still raging fiercely, although at the time of writing the services are due to end on 1 June 1981.*

In this album, I have set out to illustrate the operation of the Woodhead route under steam, diesel and electric power during recent years, and to show the diversity of traffic, motive power and scenery which the line has offered. My grateful thanks must go to all those photographers who have contributed from their collections, and from which my final selections had to be ruthlessly made due to space limitations. Last, but certainly not least, my thanks go to my wife Andrea, who has suffered my hours of absence by the lineside and in the darkroom with great patience and understanding. Several of our holiday wanderings have mysteriously ended at remote lineside locations, often in inclement weather conditions, to be followed by a seemingly endless wait for the next train to appear in the viewfinder. Together with enthusiasts from far and wide, she too will remember the Woodhead route.

---

*Actual closure was with effect from 20 July 1981.

Left: Old and new at London Road in 1940. 'D10' No 5438 ***Worsley-Taylor,*** one of Robinson's original 'Director' 4-4-0s, arrives with a train from Cleethorpes as Gresley 'B17' 4-6-0 No 2849 ***Barnsley*** prepares to depart with the 14.10 to Marylebone. *Kenneth Oldham*

Above: A Manchester (London Road)-Marylebone express passes Newton behind 'B17' 4-6-0 No 2849 ***Sheffield United***. *Kenneth Oldham*

Right: Robinson's first 4-6-0 design was the Class 8 of 1902. They were known as the 'Fish engines' due to their use on express fish trains from Grimsby. Here No 5183 passes Newton with a down freight in 1940. Known by the LNER as Class B5, they became extinct in 1950. *Kenneth Oldham*

Left: **The 'Immingham' 4-6-0s appeared in 1906, and were designed for express passenger working. Running as Class B4, and resplendent in LNER apple green, No 6102 approaches Godley with up coal empties.** *Kenneth Oldham*

Below: **Gresley Pacifics came to the line in the late 1930s. Here, Class A1 No 4474 *Victor Wild* nears Godley with an express from Marylebone in 1940.** *Kenneth Oldham*

Right: **'B17' 4-6-0 No 2869 *Barnsley* crosses Dinting Viaduct with a Manchester-Cleethorpes train in 1940. Note the platform gas lamp, which has been modified to comply with blackout regulations.** *Kenneth Oldham*

Below right: **With smokebox door glowing, 'D11' 4-4-0 No 5502 *Zeebrugge* descends past Valehouse with a Cleethorpes-Manchester train. Although the support steelwork is visible in this 1940 scene, 14 years were to pass before completion of the electrification scheme.** *Kenneth Oldham*

L N E R

Left: **Known as 'Black Pigs' or 'Miners' Friends' due to their appetite for coal, the four-cylinder ex-GCR Class 9Q 4-6-0s became LNER Class B7. No 5482 drifts towards Valehouse with a down goods.** *Kenneth Oldham*

Below left: **Wartime operating requirements humbled the mightiest express passenger locomotives. Gresley's pioneer GNR Pacific No 4470 *Great Northern*, covered in grime, nears Torside with a down goods.** *Kenneth Oldham*

Right: **An Eastbound troop special climbs the gradient near Torside behind 'Footballer' No 2861 *Sheffield Wednesday*.** *Kenneth Oldham*

Below: **The morning Liverpool-Hull train passes Torside behind Ivatt Atlantic No 4412. Points of interest here are the permanent way gang assembling their trolley, the ex-GCR 'Barnum' coach and the whitewashed buffer stop. The sheeting on the roof of No 4412 was used to hide the firebox glare from enemy aircraft.** *Kenneth Oldham*

Left: **An LMS Stanier '8F' 2-8-0 in LNER ownership, No 3515 hauls a mixed freight train near Hattersley in 1946.** *Eric Oldham*

Centre left: **The 'B7' 4-6-0s were a mixed traffic version, with 5ft 8in wheels, of the powerful 'Lord Faringdon' class. Here, No 1373 hauls eastbound coal empties past Hattersley in 1947.** *Eric Oldham*

Bottom left: **The new Thompson Class B1 4-6-0s rapidly displaced their ex-GCR counterparts. Newly-constructed 'B1' No 1158 is seen near Hattersley with a Marylebone-London Road express.** *Eric Oldham*

Top right: **Soon after nationalisation, 'C13' 4-4-2T No 67417 is seen propelling a Manchester-Glossop train near Hattersley. Note the six-wheel bogies of the leading trailer.** *Eric Oldham*

Bottom right: **'B1' 4-6-0 No 1147 leaves Mottram with a Sheffield-Manchester train in 1947. Members of this class, newly delivered from Vulcan Foundry at Newton-le-Willows, often performed their initial testing and running-in turns on this service.** *Eric Oldham*

L N E R
1183

60103
60103

Left: **Another 'B1', No 1183, enters Dinting in 1947 with a coal train made up of wooden-bodied wagons.** *Eric Oldham*

Bottom left: **Perhaps the most famous of Gresley's Pacifics, No 60103 *Flying Scotsman* prepares to depart from Manchester (London Road) with the 14.10 service to Marylebone on a summer day in 1952.** *B. K. B. Green*

Right: **The Gresley 'V2' 2-6-2s shared the express passenger workings with the 'A3' Pacifics, and here the 14.10 express to Marylebone is seen leaving London Road behind a rather grimy No 60890.** *B. K. B. Green*

Below: **The 'C13' 4-4-2T locomotives provided power for most of the local trains out of London Road prior to electrification. Nos 67401 and 67431 await departure with trains to Glossop and Macclesfield.** *K. Field*

Left: **'C13' 4-4-2T No 67437 accelerates the 09.30 London Road-Macclesfield way from Fairfield. Notice the interesting ground signal alongside the front bogie of the locomotive.**
B. K. B. Green

Below: **An eastbound express enters Guide Bridge behind LNER 'K3' 2-6-0 No 202 in September 1945. The interesting signals have long since disappeared.** *H. C. Casserley*

Right: **'C13' No 67437 makes a smoky exit from Guide Bridge with a Macclesfield train in April 1956.**
R. W. Hinton

Below right: **A long train of eastbound coal empties passes Guide Bridge behind '04/7' class 2-8-0 No 63761. These locomotives were Gresley rebuilds, with 02-type boilers, of the original Robinson '9K' 2-8-0s.** *B. K. B. Green*

Above: **The Thompson 'L1' class 2-6-4Ts operated in the Manchester area, and here No 67782 is seen pausing at Guide Bridge with a Macclesfield train in May 1959.**
C. W. Woodhead

Left: **A borrowed York-based 'B16/3', No 61464, heads towards home territory with a fitted freight, seen here at Newton.** *B. K. B. Green*

Bottom left: **Ex-GCR '04/1' No 63762 climbs steadily up the 1 in 143 through Godley with an eastbound freight. The locomotive remains in almost original '9K' form.**
B. K. B. Green

Top right: **'A3' Pacific No 60059 *Tracery* makes a fine smoke display while climbing towards Godley with the 14.10 Manchester (London Road)-Marylebone express in 1953.** *B. K. B. Green*

Right: **With steam to spare, 'K2/2' class 2-6-0 No 61751 nears Godley with an up fitted freight.**
B. K. B. Green

61751

63614

48709

Left: **An up freight clears Godley East Junction behind '04/1' class 2-8-0 No 63614 in May 1953.** *R. W. Hinton*

Below left: **Stanier '8F' 2-8-0 No 48709 takes the Stockport line at Godley Junction with a freight for the Liverpool area.** *D. Birch*

Right: **Almost at the end of regular steam operation, 'K3' 2-6-0 No 61828 hurries past Mottram with a down express in June 1954.** *T. Lewis (N. E. Preedy Collection)*

Below: **Two vintage coaches forming the 14.22 Glossop-Dinting are propelled towards the terminus by 'C13' 4-4-2T No 67421.** *B. K. B. Green*

63876

Left: **Class 04/7 2-8-0 No 63876 drifts downhill through wintry surroundings near Valehouse with a westbound coal train.** *B. K. B. Green*

Below left: **Work on the new tunnel is nearing completion as Class 02/3 2-8-0 No 63987 emerges from the down single bore at Woodhead with a coal train.** *B. K. B. Green*

Right: **A sight which must have gladdened the hearts of countless engine crews – the view from the summit of the eastbound climb to Dunford Bridge, just inside the up tunnel.** *H. C. Casserley*

Below: **Towards the end of steam haulage, westbound from Sheffield 'A3' Pacific No 60104 *Solario* approaches Dunford Bridge with the 07.32 Leicester Central-Manchester London Road.** *B. K. B. Green*

250

64343
64343

Left: **Class B1 4-6-0 No 61114 pounds through Hazelhead with a special from Barnsley to Manchester.** *B. K. B. Green*

Below left: **Carrying express passenger headlamps, 'Pom-Pom' Class J11 0-6-0 No 64343 pilots ex-LMS '4MT' 2-6-0 No 43114 through Thurlstone with a Rotherham-Hyde excursion.**
B. K. B. Green

Top right: **The Harwich-Liverpool service was one of the Woodhead route's most well known services. 'B1' 4-6-0 No 61223 passes Thurlstone signal box with the down train in this 1953 view.**
B. K. B. Green

Centre right: **An up train comprising ex-GCR stock of varying ages descends towards Sheffield past Wharncliffe Wood behind an immaculate 'D9' 4-4-0 No 5041 piloting 'J11' No 5983.**
Blencowe Collection

Below: **A view looking in the opposite direction. A down local made up of vintage clerestory-roofed stock passes Wharncliffe Wood signal box behind 'C13' 4-4-2T No 6058.** *Blencowe Collection*

Above: **During the last days of the LNER, 'B1' 4-6-0 No 1161 climbs through sylvan surroundings towards Penistone with an express for Manchester.** *C. B. Harley*

Left: **Two Class 04 2-8-0s wait in sidings at Beeley Wood, near Wadsley Bridge, as 'B1' 4-6-0 No 61179 passes with the Harwich-Liverpool train on a winter's day in 1953.** *P. Hughes*

Above right: **Wath marshalling yard was built in early GCR days to cope with cross-Pennine freight traffic. In this busy scene, an '04/1' 2-8-0 awaits departure eastwards as Doncaster-based '02/3' No 63974 enters with an express freight.** *P. Hughes*

Right: **No 9902 was one of the three original three-cylinder 0-8-4T engines produced specifically for operation in Wath yard. In this view it carries its original GC chimney and wartime abbreviated 'NE' initials.** *P. Hughes*

63974

N E
9902

Top: One of the ex-GCR 0-8-0 'Tinies', later LNER class Q4, No 3219, grinds up Wentworth incline with rear end assistance from an '04' 2-8-0 and the Beyer-Garratt Class U1 2-8-8-2 No 9999. *H. C. Casserley*

Above: In pouring rain during April 1947, '04/8' No 3672 and Garratt No 9999 assist a coal train up Wentworth incline. *H. C. Casserley*

Top right: The Garratt at rest between banking turns. Although designed for high availability, its working life was hindered by constantly leaking joints in the steam pipes from the boiler to the front and rear chassis units. *H. C. Casserley*

Right: Prior to completion of the Wath-Penistone electrification in 1952, No 69999 was tried on banking duties in the Lickey Incline, working from Bromsgrove. These proved unsuccessful, and the locomotive returned to Manchester for trials with heavy freight trains on the eastbound climb to Woodhead tunnel. In 1955 it was converted to oil burning, and is seen here in rebuilt form while pausing for steam at Hadfield. *B. K. B. Green*

9999

69999

Above: **The oil-burning trials continued during 1955, but were not judged successful. During this period No 69999 was caught by the camera, near Newton with a freight on the way to the summit. It was withdrawn from service at the end of the year.** *B. K. B. Green*

Left: **Westbound from Sheffield, trains generally made the climb to Woodhead without assistance. '04/1' No 63587 tackles the 1 in 132 to Oughtybridge with a down coal train.** *P. Hughes*

Above: The locomotive exchanges of 1948 found ex-SR 'West Country' class 4-6-2 No 34006 *Bude* performing test runs over the GCR main line to Manchester. In order to make use of the water troughs on LMR routes, an LMS 8F tender was fitted. The locomotive is seen here in SR livery but with BR numbers awaiting departure from Sheffield Victoria. The first vehicle is the North Eastern dynamometer car. *P. Hughes*

Right: A Westbound coal train made up of modern steel-bodied wagons clears Wadsley Bridge station behind '04/3' 2-8-0 No 63842. This was one of the locomotives built for the Railway Operating Department of the Army and used on overseas service from 1917. *P. Hughes*

·63574·
63574

42437

Left: **'04/1' No 63574, of Darnall shed, at Sheffield Victoria about to work a local train to Penistone. Note, behind the tender, an unusual van believed to be of Midland origin, followed by an ex-SR van, examples of which are still in service in 1980.** *B. N. Cooper*

Below left: **Leicester Central-based 2-6-4T No 42437 awaits departure for home with an evening local from Sheffield.** *J. H. Turner*

Above: **Another view of the up 'Continental', showing 'B17/6' No 61633 *Kimbolton Castle* awaiting departure.** *B. K. B. Green*

Centre right: **'D11/1' No 62661 *Gerard Powys Dewhurst* awaits departure from Victoria with a stopping train for Leicester. Grime and old age could not hide the dignity and impressive lines of the 'Large Directors'.** *J. H. Turner*

Bottom right: **Although not heading for Woodhead, this fine shot of a well-cleaned 'D11' had to be included. No 62666 *Zeebrugge* steps smartly away from Sheffield with the 10.05 for Nottingham on Good Friday, 1957.** *K. S. Hudson*

Left: **Work started on the new Woodhead tunnel in February 1949. The project is well in hand in this view of the Dunford Bridge end, showing a 'J39' 0-6-0 grinding up the last few yards to the summit.** *P. Ransome-Wallis*

Below: **'EM1' Bo-Bo No 26040 is seen here as the first locomotive to enter the still incomplete depot at Reddish, Manchester, on 4 May 1954. Several months were to elapse before the depot was completed.** *B. K. B. Green*

Right: **The pioneer 'EM1' No 26000** ***Tommy,*** **seen at Reddish. Note the front end differences from other members of the class.** *B. K. B. Green*

Below right: **The crew of 'C13' No 67431 study the first of the new 1,500v dc emus working out of London Road on the Glossop service on 18 May 1954.** *B. K. B. Green*

26000
TOMMY
26000

GLOSSOP

Left: **The old down tunnel is out of service, and one track out of the new tunnel has been connected into the existing down line. A string of light engines headed by '04/6' No 63848 work wrong line towards Manchester.** *B. K. B. Green*

Below: **Nos 26016 and 26001 became the first electric locos to operate under their own power through the tunnel, on 30 May 1954. In this view they are about to enter the tunnel at Woodhead.** *B. K. B. Green*

Right: **A view of the Woodhead end of the tunnels, taken shortly before completion of the works.** *British Railways*

Below right: **No 26020, now preserved in the National Railway Museum at York, officially opens the tunnel at Woodhead on 3 June 1954.** *PA-Reuter Photos Ltd*

Top: For the opening ceremony, a special train was run from Sheffield Victoria to Dunford Bridge to connect with a three-car emu, which then took passengers on a return trip through the tunnel. Here, the steam-hauled train stands in the old down platform and a walkway has been laid across the new up line. This was one of very few occasions when emus worked beyond Hadfield. *P. Hughes*

Above: Dinting viaduct during the steam/electric changeover period. An up goods hauled by an '04/1' passes a down train in the charge of an 'EM1' and an '04/7'. *B. K. B. Green*

Top right: No 26002 and an '04/1' pass Dinting with a down goods. The 'EM1' would have been attached at Penistone to allow the '04' to shut off steam while in the new tunnel, so avoiding damage to the Portland cement lining. *B. K. B. Green*

Right: The Type EM2 Co-Cos at 2,500hp were more powerful than the 'EM1' type and were produced specifically for passenger train operation. No 27004 leaves London Road with an express for Marylebone. *E. Treacy*

27004

Top left: **Soon after the introduction of full electric haulage between London Road and Victoria, 'EM1' No 26055 (later named *Prometheus*) emerges from the new tunnel at Dunford Bridge with the late-running 16.00 Manchester-Marylebone express. Although intended primarily for freight service, the Bo-Bos found plenty of work on passenger services.** *E. D. Bruton*

Centre left: **In pouring rain, 'EM1' No 26042 approaches Dunford (East) with an up train of coal empties in June 1954. Notice the immaculately-trimmed ballast below the down line.** *E. D. Bruton*

Bottom: **Better weather is evident as No 26055 descends through Torside with a down coal train in May 1955.** *T. Lewis/N. E. Preedy Collection*

Top right: **'EM2' No 27003 passes Torside with the Liverpool-Harwich express on 17 March 1956. The original British Railways black livery was perhaps the most attractive finish for these impressive machines.** *T. Lewis/N. E. Preedy Collection*

Bottom right: **On the same day, the Harwich-Liverpool train is seen passing Torside behind 'EM2' No 27002.** *R. W. Hinton*

27003

27002

MOTTRAM

WOODHEAD

Above left: **No 26016 passes No 26053 *Perseus* in a spot of bother at the outlet from Mottram Yard.** *J. Clarke*

Left: **An early railtour over the Woodhead route. The Ian Allan 'Pennine Pullman' emerges from the tunnel behind 'EM2' No 27002 on 12 May 1956.** *T. Lewis/N. E. Preedy Collection*

Above: **A scheme to run emus through from London Road to Victoria was put forward, but never materialised. A test train enters Penistone on 20 September 1957 and passes the Electric Traction Control Centre at the Western end of the station.** *B. K. B. Green*

Right: **The LNER provided a new single bore tunnel at Thurgoland when geological problems prevented the original tunnel being opened out. No 27000 emerges from the original up tunnel with a local from Penistone to Sheffield.** *K. Field*

Above: **'EM2s' Nos 27004 and 27001 stand on the centre road at Sheffield Victoria, awaiting their next turns of duty.** *B. N. Cooper*

Left: **A down express departs from Victoria behind 'EM2' No 27005.** *B. N. Cooper*

Above right: **The RCTS 'South Yorkshireman No 2' railtour of 7 June 1953 provided the freight-only Worsborough line with a rare passenger working. Here 'J11' 0-6-0 No 64374 has brought the train to Elsecar Junction, where No 26013 is coupled up for the run to Penistone.** *E. D. Bruton*

Right: **Later in the day, 26013 prepares to leave the train at Wombwell Main Junction, whilst 'D11' class 4-4-0 No 62667** ***Somme*** **is ready to take the train towards Mexborough.** *E. D. Bruton*

RCTS
26013

62667

Above: **A rare steam railtour under the wires. Restored 'A3' Pacific No 4472 *Flying Scotsman* returns to her old haunts with the SLS 'Great Central Railtour' of 18 April 1964, seen here entering Victoria in the up direction.** *P. Cookson*

Left: **During the period when the 'EM2s' carried nameplates, No 27002 *Aurora* prepares to leave the recently renamed Manchester Piccadilly station with the 19.10 to Sheffield in December 1963.** *J. Clarke*

Top right: **Diesel power on the 'Continental' in July 1964. English Electric Type 3 (now Class 37) No D6701 takes the up train, now working from Manchester only, past Torside.** *J. Clarke*

Centre right: **Shortly afterwards, 'EM2' No 27002 *Aurora* passes with the 15.10 Piccadilly-Victoria local. The experimental rotary windshield wipers were not fitted to all the 'EM2' locomotives.** *J. Clarke*

Bottom right: **Bearing yellow end-panels, an 'EM1' brings a down freight through Guide Bridge in February 1970.** *M. Dunnett*

1E 78

Left: Some of the 'EM1s' (soon to be reclassified Class 76) were modified for working in multiple from 1969 onwards, but several locos remained in original form. Un-modified No 76.049 hurries an up train of coal empties through Guide Bridge. *S. R. Batty*

Below: The cab-front jumper connections are clearly seen in this view of three mu-equipped pairs at Guide Bridge. Nos 76.033 and 76.035 enter the station with westbound steel flats. *S. R. Batty*

Right: Merry-go-round coal traffic between the Yorkshire coalfield and Fiddler's Ferry power station, near Warrington, has formed a large proportion of the line's traffic since 1970. Class 47 Co-Co No 47.338 passes Brookfield, at Godley Junction, with a train of mgr empties for the exchange sidings. From here, a Class 76 locomotive will take the train eastwards. *S. R. Batty*

Below right: Some mgr trains change traction at Mottram, south of Dinting. No 47.336 takes the ex-CLC line at Godley Junction with a loaded mgr train for Fiddler's Ferry. *S. R. Batty*

GODLEY JUNCTION

Left: **Activity at Hattersley. Permanent way staff stand clear as English Electric Class 40 No 40.098 passes by with ballast empties.** *S. R. Batty*

Below: **A sand train hurries eastwards through the freshly-scrubbed Broadbottom station, hauled by two rather less-sparkling 76s.** *S. R. Batty*

Right: **Two views of Mottram yard; here No 76.047 hauls a train of empties past the western end of the yard, alongside the electrified exit from the sidings . . .** *S. R. Batty*

. . . and looking eastwards, 76.047 passes the reception point for much of the mgr traffic. Class 47 No 47.227 prepares to depart for Fiddlers Ferry. *S. R. Batty*

Top left: **A Class 47 slowly moves a 1400-ton mgr train out of the exchange sidings and across Mottram viaduct.** *S. R. Batty*

Centre and below: **Morning and evening; the first westbound train of the day crosses Dinting viaduct on an early Spring morning in 1980 . . .** *S. R. Batty*

. . . and an up parcels train crosses the viaduct on a Summer evening in 1976. *M. Walker*

Top right: **An emu (now known as Class 506) enters Dinting station on its journey to Hadfield. The train will reverse at Glossop, return to Dinting and continue to Hadfield.** *S. R. Batty*

Bottom right: **Only in very recent years has the line carried a significant number of railtours. The 'Pennine Explorer' of 14 October 1978 pauses at Dinting behind Nos 76.016 and 76.003.** *N. E. Preedy*

M59401M

PENNINE
EXPLORER
76016
12
10

Above: **At Valehouse, east of Hadfield, up trains face a slight easing of the climb from 1 in 100 to 1 in 117. No 76.049 passes the box with coal empties for Rotherwood.** *S. R. Batty*

Left: **Oil tank empties pass the down loop exit at Valehouse behind No 76.035. The use of an mu fitted locomotive on a 'single' load is uncommon.** *S. R. Batty*

Below left: **From Bramah Edge, almost 700ft above the railway at Torside, fine views of Longendale are available. Two 76s approach Torside crossing with up mgr empties.** *S. R. Batty*

Right: **During the last month of passenger services a chilly moorland scene surrounds a Class 76 heading eastwards near Torside. Five coaches was the standard load on this service.** *K. Groundwater*

Above left: **Very little road traffic is inconvenienced by railway operations at the lonely Torside crossing. Nos 76.008 and 76.029 cross the deserted road with a down mgr train in October 1979.** *S. R. Batty*

Left: **An eastbound empties train crosses Wildboard Clough, on the climb to Crowden.** *S. R. Batty*

Above: **Nos 76.012 and 76.014 slow to a stop at Woodhead, owing to line occupation ahead at Penistone. The catenary supports are still standing in the site of the former sidings, now dominated by the National Grid 400Kv pylons.** *S. R. Batty*

Right: **Nos 76.011 and 76.025 rattle a train of empty steel flats towards Woodhead tunnel.** *S. R. Batty*

Left: **No 76.001 is about to plunge into the tunnel with a train of eastbound empties. The cable troughing on the right is laid on the site of the original tunnel tracks and the station buildings.** *S. R. Batty*

Bottom left: **In 1963 the CEGB decided to use the former up tunnel to carry a 400,000 volt power line from Dunford to Woodhead. A 2ft gauge railway was laid through the bore for construction and maintenance purposes, and is clearly visible in this view as No 76.049 emerges from the new tunnel with a down coal train. Both 400kV circuits were energised in October 1969.** *S. R. Batty*

Top right: **The cable-cooling-water pumping station at Woodhead. The former down tunnel is available as a fire exit via the cross-headings if necessary. Soot deposits up to 9in thick were removed from the up tunnel during renovation.** *S. R. Batty*

Bottom right: **Old and new tunnel approaches at Dunford Bridge. Remains of the original platform and station buildings can be seen.** *S. R. Batty*

Left: **In fine Spring weather, two Class 76s haul steel empties eastwards from Dunford Bridge towards Penistone.** *S. R. Batty*

***Centre left:* No E26054 *Pluto*, in ex-works condition, passes Hazelhead with the 14.10 Manchester Piccadilly-Sheffield Victoria in September 1969.** *P. A. Hogarth*

***Bottom:* Traffic from the Hope Valley route is often diverted via Woodhead to allow engineering work to take place. The Sunday 09.25 Liverpool-Sheffield, formed by vehicles of one of the Swindon-built 'Trans-Pennine' dmu sets, passes Hazelhead on one such occasion in 1980.** *S. R. Batty*

***Top right:* Another railtour, this time diesel-hauled; the 'Class 44 Farewell' tour of 21 January 1978 passes Hazelhead behind No 44.009 *Snowdon*.** *L. A. Nixon*

***Bottom right:* In BR lined green livery No E26000 *Tommy* hauls the 14.45 Victoria-Piccadilly round Bullhouse Curve in July, 1969.** *P. A. Hogarth*

FAREWELL
44

Left: **The same location over ten years later, showing a Class 123 'Inter-City' dmu forming the 08.15 Sheffield-Manchester diverted from the Hope Valley line. Note the disappearance of the former down loop and realignment of tracks.** *S. R. Batty*

Centre left: **Dusk gathers as Nos 76.035 and 76.037 pass Shore Hall crossing with up steel empties.** *S. R. Batty*

Bottom: **On a fine winter morning, the peace at Shore Hall is shattered by No 47.443 heading the late-running and diverted 09.45 Manchester-St. Pancras towards Penistone.** *S. R. Batty*

Top right: **In the snows of 1979 an up sand train passes Thurlstone behind Nos 76.009 and 76.025.** *S. R. Batty*

Bottom right: **A former Trans-Pennine dmu set, reduced to a four-car formation, passes Penistone (Goods) on the diverted 09.25 Liverpool Lime Street-Sheffield (Midland) in January, 1980.** *S. R. Batty*

Above left: **No 26001 enters Penistone with an up train of steel empties on a damp day in March, 1970.**
J. H. Cooper-Smith

Left: **A sudden blizzard has descended on Penistone as Nos 76.034 and 76.039 pass Huddersfield Junction with westbound empty oil tanks.** *S. R. Batty*

Above: **The eastern end of Penistone station, showing the Huddersfield platform curving northwards.**
S. R. Batty

Below: **An early morning view of Penistone, with the 06.10 dmu from Huddersfield about to cross the viaduct and enter the station.** *S. R. Batty*

Left: **Coal traffic from Dodworth Colliery, near Barnsley, is handed over to electric traction at Penistone. Here, Class 45 1Co-Co1 No 45.036 passes Barnsley Junction with a return train of empties.** *S. R. Batty*

Centre left: **Class 47 No 47.483 accelerates the diverted 09.45 Manchester Piccadilly-St Pancras past Blackmoor Crossing, east of Penistone.** *S. R. Batty*

Bottom: **A late-running, diverted 07.50 St Pancras-Manchester Piccadilly passes Oxspring behind Class 45 No 45.125.** *S. R. Batty*

Top right: ***Tommy*** **again, this time crossing Rumtickle viaduct, Thurgoland, with the 14.45 Victoria-Piccadilly in July 1969.** *P. A. Hogarth*

Bottom right: **Class 40 1Co-Co1 No 40.116 passes Deepcar, hauling a dead 'Trans-Pennine' dmu from Newton Heath for repairs at Botanic Gardens depot, Hull. On the left is the ground frame controlling access to Stocksbridge Steelworks.** *S. R. Batty*

DEEPCAR
DONCASTER

Left: **A football special passes Deepcar behind Class 40 No 40.108 on its return from Wadsley Bridge to Liverpool. Wrong line working is in force due to a freight train derailment near Oughtybridge.** *S. R. Batty*

Below left: **The diverted 12.45 Manchester Piccadilly-Doncaster passes the remains of Deepcar station. The goods yard is still used for some local coal traffic.** *S. R. Batty*

Right: **Nos 76.021 and 76.013 pause at Wadsley Bridge with the 'AC-DC' railtour of 16 September 1978.** *N. E. Preedy*

Below: **A weekend view of Rotherwood sidings, Sheffield, showing eight Class 76s, all mu-fitted, awaiting their next turns of duty.** *S. R. Batty*

76008
76 029

Left: **A close view of the cab and end details of two locomotives working in multiple. On No 76.029 the previous number (E26029) is faintly discernible, and this locomotive is also somewhat lower on its suspension. Note the traditional sand boxes and also the different axleboxes, that on the left, carrying a speedometer drive cable. Both locomotives have lost their oval builder's plates.** *S. R. Batty*

Below left: **Returning to the Worsborough line, Nos 76.009 and 76.023 are seen crossing Oxspring viaduct, near Barnsley junction, with a westbound steel train.** *S. R. Batty*

Right: **The Oughtybridge derailment of early 1980 resulted in the Huddersfield and Sheffield service being diverted for some time via Silkstone and Barnsley. A dmu is here seen entering Oxspring tunnel with a Sheffield train.** *S. R. Batty*

Below: **The diverted 11.32 Sheffield-Huddersfield passes West Silkstone junction. On the right can be seen the start of the 1 in 40 descent to Wentworth.** *S. R. Batty*

20

Left: **The view westwards as two '76's cautiously cross over and prepare to descend the incline with a train of empties.** *S. R. Batty*

Below left: **Nos 76.011 and 76.012 grind up the last few yards to the summit of the 1 in 40 with a 1400ton mgr train. A brief stop will be made to detach the banking locomotives.** *S. R. Batty*

Top right: **Having uncoupled their locomotives from the train, the banking crew prepare to cross over and return to Wombwell.** *S. R. Batty*

Centre right: **Some detail for modellers. West Silkstone Junction signalbox, despite some loose slates, absence of handrail, and frost-damaged brickwork, still looks reasonably smart.** *S. R. Batty*

Bottom right: **Nos 76.022 and 76.013 about to enter the longer of the two Silkstone tunnels on the return to Wombwell. Note the British Railways lion emblem on No 76.022.** *S. R. Batty*

Left and below: **Coal from Dodworth colliery is hurried towards West Silkstone behind Class 37 Co-Co No 37.226 . . .**

. . . and a little later, 37.226 returns with mgr empties. *Both S. R. Batty*

Right: **Nos 76.024 and 76.015 reach the foot of the 1 in 40 descent at the remains of Wentworth Junction. The lifted connection to the original line is seen on the left.** *S. R. Batty*

Below right: **Steel empties descend to Wombwell past Lewden Crossing, behind Nos 76.026/7, amid the bleak winter scenery of March 1979.**
S. R. Batty

Left: Nos 76.032 and 76.033, with a train of mgr empties, pass under the Leeds-Barnsley-Sheffield line at Wombwell. *S. R. Batty*

Below: A westbound steel train pauses at Wombwell while the banker buffers up to provide assistance for the climb to West Silkstone. Two mu-fitted bankers are available for use on 'double-load' trains. The line in the foreground is the ex-GCR Wombwell-Sheffield line, now serving only collieries at Worsborough and Hoyland. *S. R. Batty*

Right: In more favourable weather, an up freight pauses to allow its pilot (not mu-fitted) to draw clear at Wombwell. This is an unusual combination, probably adopted for operating convenience. *S. R. Batty*

Below right: Nos 76.021 and 76.008 negotiate the curve at Wombwell Main with steel empties. *S. R. Batty*

Above: **At Aldam Junction the electrified line leaves the Mexborough-Barnsley line after its short journey from Wath. Two 76s pass the junction with coal empties for Wath yard.** *S. R. Batty*

Below: **Early morning mist clears from Barnsley Junction.**
S. R. Batty